At a Party

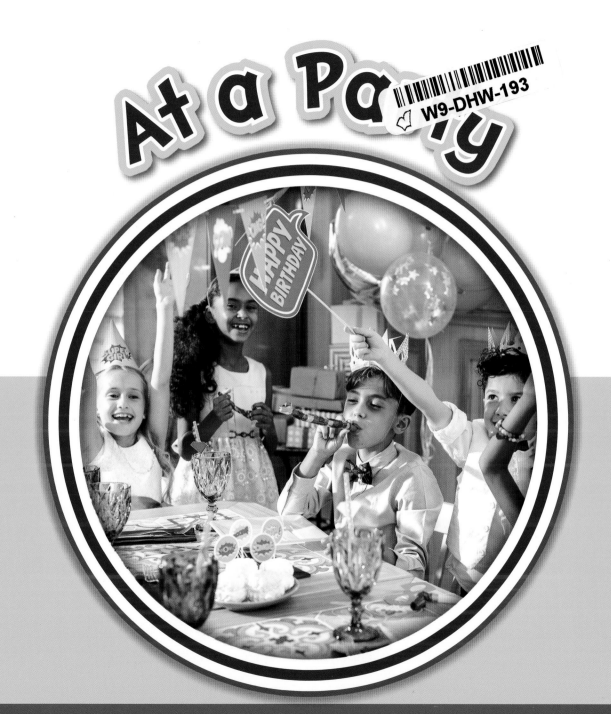

BY ALYSSA KREKELBERG

At a party, children play with friends.

At a party, children play with toys.

At a party, children play games.

At a party, children
eat food at a table.

At a party, children sing "Happy Birthday."

At a party, children
eat birthday cake.

At a party, children
give presents.

At a party, the birthday girl opens presents.

At a party, the birthday girl gets a toy.

At a party, children
are happy.

Note to Caregivers and Educators

Sight words are a foundation for reading. It's important for young readers to have sight words memorized at a glance without breaking them down into individual letter sounds. Sight words are often phonetically irregular and can't be sounded out, so readers need to memorize them. Knowing sight words allows readers to focus on more difficult words in the text. The intent of this book is to repeat specific sight words as many times as possible throughout the story. Through repetition of the words, emerging readers will recognize, and ideally memorize, each sight word. Memorizing sight words can help improve readers' literacy skills.

a

at

party

About the Author

Alyssa Krekelberg is a children's
book editor and author. She
lives in Minnesota and enjoys
exploring the great outdoors with
her hyper husky.

Published by The Child's World®
1980 Lookout Drive • Mankato, MN 56003-1705
800-599-READ • www.childsworld.com

Photographs ©: iStockphoto, cover, 1, 2, 5, 6, 9, 10, 13, 14, 17, 18, 21, 23

ISBN 9781503835597
LCCN 2019943118

Printed in the United States of America